BEGINNER'S GUIDE TO
Bicycling &
Bike Maintenance

Tony Lawler
Illustrated by Clive Spong
and Jonathan Langley

Designed by Sharon Martin
Series editor: Lisa Watts

Contents

First published in 1980 by Usborne Publishing Ltd, 20 Garrick Street, London WC2E 9BJ, England.
Copyright © 1980 Usborne Publishing Ltd

Printed in Spain

The name Usborne and the device ☺ are Trade Marks of Usborne Publishing Ltd.

How to use this book

This book is a basic guide to cycling and looking after a bicycle. Clear and simple step-by-step pictures and instructions show how to do basic maintenance jobs such as oiling the bike and mending a puncture, and there are lots of ideas for cycle tours, races and cycling competitions.

To find out how to do a particular maintenance job, such as fitting new brakes or adjusting the pedals, look it up in the index. Then turn to the right page and follow the picture-by-picture instructions.

At the beginning of the book there are hints for safe cycling and special guidelines for riding in cities. When you are riding on roads, always be very careful, and if you do any of the races or games in this book, choose a quiet place where there is no traffic.

You need to clean and grease the parts of a bike about twice a year to keep it in good working order. The maintenance section of this book shows how to do this and how to take the bike apart and put it together again.

If your bike is not working well, but you are not sure what is wrong, turn to the fault-finding guide on pages 60–62. These pages will show you what the problem is, and how to put it right.

3

Types of bike

If you are thinking of buying a bike, first decide what sort of cycling you will be doing most. You need a different sort of bike for short trips with lots of luggage than for long-distance cycling.

If you buy a second-hand bike, check it for rust and make sure the wheels and frame are not bent. The maintenance section in this book shows how to make an old bike roadworthy.

Tourers

MAN'S VERSION HAS CROSSBAR

These have straight handlebars so you ride sitting upright*. They generally have three-speed gears.

Small wheel bikes

LARGE SADDLE-BAG

These have lots of space above the wheels for carrying shopping. You ride in the upright position.

Roadsters

ROD BRAKES

These are strong, but heavy bikes. They have straight handlebars, rod brakes and three-speed gears.

Fun bikes

SMALL WHEELS

Sometimes called "choppers" these have tall handlebars, heavy-tread tyres and three- or four-speed gears.

Sports bikes

TEN-SPEED GEARS

Lightweight bikes with large wheels, five- or ten-speed gears and dropped handlebars. Good for speed and long distances.

*You can fit dropped bars to a tourer, see page 31.

Adjusting the  bike to fit you

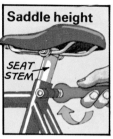

Saddle height

SEAT STEM

When you sit on your bike the saddle should be positioned so you can just touch the ground and the handlebars so that you are leaning on them slightly.

Loosen bolt on seat stem, slide saddle up or down. Tighten bolt.

Handlebars

EXPANDER BOLT

To alter the height, unscrew expander bolt 25mm. Tap down with a mallet, or cover with a bit of wood and use a hammer.

Hold the front wheel between your knees and raise or lower the handlebars. Screw up bolt until firm, but not too tight.

If your knees are too near the handlebars you can move the saddle back, or tilt the handlebars forward a bit.

To move the seat loosen the nut underneath. To tilt handlebars, loosen bolt as shown. Tighten both again.

Basic equipment

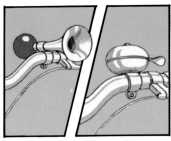

For cycling at night you must have lights. They can be battery lamps, or dynamos, which are charged as you pedal.

You should have a bell or horn on your bike so you can ring or hoot if people or animals are in your way.

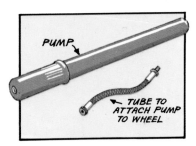

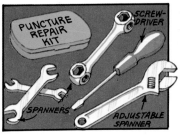

Never go out without a bicycle pump. If you get a puncture you can keep pumping up the tyre until you can fix it.

You should also carry a few tools with you on your bike, and a puncture-mending kit for emergency repairs.

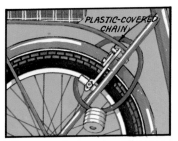

For carrying things you need a saddle-bag, or a basket. Never hang things from the handlebars as this spoils your balance.

When you leave your bike you should put a chain and padlock through the wheel and frame, and chain it to a post or railing.*

*Take off the pump and anything else that could be stolen too.

Cycling clothes

When you are cycling you will probably have more trouble keeping cool than warm. It is best to wear several layers of clothing, such as a shirt, jumper and jacket, so you can take off the top layers as you get hot.

Make sure the clothes you wear are safe. If they are very loose they could flap and get in your way, or get caught in the wheels or chain.

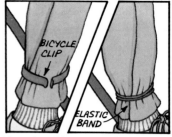

You should secure wide trousers round your ankles with bicycle clips, elastic bands or tuck them in your socks.

Flat shoes with firm soles are best for cycling so you can pedal firmly.

A hat and gloves are good as your head and hands may get cold.

A jacket with a front zip keeps you warm – and can be opened when you get hot.

For cycling in the rain you can get a cycle cape quite cheaply. This keeps your body, legs and arms dry.

So that you can easily be seen it is a good idea to wear coloured bands which shine in the dark. You can buy them in cycle shops.

Learning to ride

If possible, find a place that is flat, with lots of space and no traffic. Before you leave home, check that the handlebars and saddle are the right height for you. It is best to wear trousers, jacket and gloves to protect you in case you fall off.

PEDAL UP →

Start with one foot on the ground and the other on the pedal. Make sure this pedal is in its highest position.

Push the pedal down, lift your other foot up and pedal with both feet. Turn the handlebars gently to help you balance.

Keep pedalling so you build up speed. It is hard to balance if you go too slowly.

BACK BRAKE

Squeeze the back brake just before the front so you do not skid.

LEAN THIS WAY

Lean slightly into corners to help you balance.

Balance practice

Somewhere where there is no traffic put some old cans and cycle between them.

Draw two chalk lines 50cm apart and try to cycle between them.

Practise riding along and glancing quickly behind you, without wobbling.

Hand signals

You should practise these until you can do them without wobbling. To turn right, stick out your right arm.

To turn left, put your left arm out. To show you are slowing down, wave your right arm slowly up and down.

Road signs

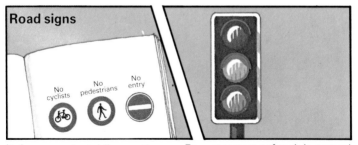

Before you start riding on the roads, you should learn what all the road signs mean.

For your own safety it is a good idea to take a cycling course. You can find out about these from your local library.

Out on the road

When you are out cycling you should concentrate all the time and be very alert. Watch the other traffic and be ready to brake or turn if necessary.

It is also important to keep your bike in a good condition – especially the brakes and tyres.

Before you move out from the kerb, and before you turn right or left, or overtake, you must look behind you to make sure there are no cars coming.

Turning right

Look behind, then, unless a car is about to overtake, signal with your right arm.

Move to the centre of the road and stop to make sure there are no cars coming.

When the road is clear, turn right. Stay on the correct side of the road.

Turning left

Look behind you and if it is safe, put your left hand out to signal.

Make sure there are no cars coming. If there are, stop at the junction.

When it is clear, turn left, keeping close to the kerb.

Road sense

Keep a good distance from the car in front of you, in case it should suddenly stop. If you are riding with friends, you should ride single file, not side-by-side.

Stay near the kerb, but not too close or you will be riding over the drains.

Watch out for people who may not hear you coming. Ring your bell or shout to warn them.

It is illegal to ride at night without lights. You should have a white light on the front of the bike and a red one on the back.

In the rain your brakes will not work as quickly as when they are dry, so you must give yourself longer to stop.

Never take any risks. If there is a lot of traffic you can always get off and push your bike till the road is clear.

City cycling

You have to be extra careful and alert when riding in towns and cities. Often drivers just do not notice a cyclist. Watch out, especially when you are turning left, that a car turning at the same time does not cut in on you.

Remember, all the road signs apply to you as well as to the motorist. You should not cycle the wrong way down one-way streets and should stop for people at crossings.

Choosing your route

Plan your route carefully and see if you can avoid traffic jams and busy roads by riding through a park or back street.

SHORT CUT

Look out, too, for short cuts down paths and passages. You may not be allowed to cycle, but you can always push your bike.

Since you do not go as fast as the cars, keep to the kerb side of the road.

Watch out

FUMES

If you see fumes coming from a car's exhaust it may be about to pull out.

MOVING WHEELS

If the wheels of a parked car are turning, the car is probably about to move.

DOOR OPENING

Be ready to shout or swerve if you see a car door opening in front of you.

How to use gears

If you have gears on your bike it is much easier to pedal up hills. There are two main types of gears — hub gears which are usually three-speed, and derailleur (pronounced *dee-ray-lee-uh*) gears which have five or ten different speeds.

GEAR LEVER FOR HUB GEARS

With hub gears you stop pedalling when you change gear with derailleur gears you pedal as you change.

Use a low gear (L or 1 on hub gears) for going up hill. Change gear as you come to the hill, before pedalling gets too hard.

You can also get more power by standing on the pedals, but be careful as you have less control when you ride like this.

In town, start off in low gear (hub gears L or 1), then, as you pick up speed change to a higher gear (H or 3).

13

Parts of a bike

This picture shows the names of the main parts of a bike. Your bike may look a bit different from this one, but it will still have these parts.

If you want to find out more about a particular part of the bike, turn to the page number in brackets after the name.

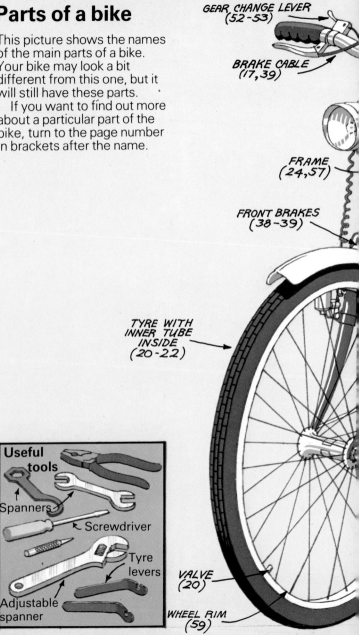

GEAR CHANGE LEVER
(52-53)

BRAKE CABLE
(17,39)

FRAME
(24,57)

FRONT BRAKES
(38-39)

TYRE WITH
INNER TUBE
INSIDE
(20-22)

Useful tools

Spanners

Screwdriver

Tyre levers

Adjustable spanner

VALVE
(20)

WHEEL RIM
(59)

14

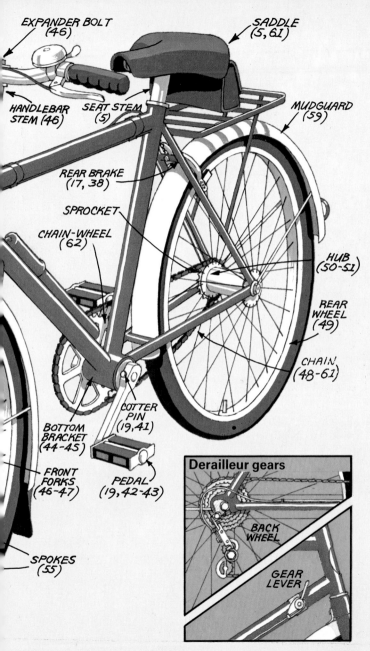

EXPANDER BOLT (46)

SADDLE (5, 61)

HANDLEBAR STEM (46)

SEAT STEM (5)

MUDGUARD (59)

REAR BRAKE (17, 38)

SPROCKET

CHAIN-WHEEL (62)

HUB (50-51)

REAR WHEEL (49)

CHAIN (48-61)

COTTER PIN (19,41)

BOTTOM BRACKET (44-45)

FRONT FORKS (46-47)

PEDAL (19,42-43)

SPOKES (55)

Derailleur gears

BACK WHEEL

GEAR LEVER

15

Cleaning and looking after a bike

To keep your bike in good condition you should clean it regularly, so the moving parts do not get clogged with dirt and grease. As you clean you can look out for loose or worn parts which need attention.

Useful things for cleaning are rags and sponges and an old toothbrush. To remove thick grease you can use paraffin*, or a degreaser which you can buy at hardware shops or garages.

PLASTIC BAG

Turn the bike upside down to work on it, and wrap the handlebars and saddle in plastic bags to protect them.

Brush the bike with paraffin (or degreaser) to remove very thick dirt, but do not put it on the wheel hubs or bottom bracket.

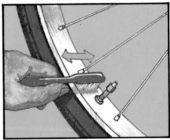

Use an old toothbrush to clean between the spokes of the wheels, and other places that are hard to get at.

Wash off the paraffin or degreaser with soap and water, and use this to clean the bottom bracket and wheel hubs.

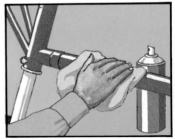

Dry the bike with a cloth then polish paintwork with furniture polish and clean chrome with chrome polish.

16   *Remember, paraffin is inflammable.*

A bike, like a car, needs regular maintenance to keep it in good working order. Each time you go out you should check the brakes and tyres. You should also oil the bike regularly and check for loose parts. The places to oil are shown on pages 18–19.

Tyres

If you can press the tyre in it needs more air. Take the dustcap off the valve, screw on the pump adaptor, then screw the pump to the other end of the adaptor.

Stand comfortably and pump slowly and regularly until the tyre is as hard as you can get it. Remember to replace dustcap.

Wheels

Check your wheels to see if they wobble. If they do, you need to tighten the cone nuts (see pages 48–49) with a spanner.

Brakes

Brake blocks should be about 3mm from the wheel rim. To move them closer tighten the adjuster screw.

Make sure the blocks touch only the wheel rim and not the tyre. To slide a block up or down a bit, loosen the nut shown here.

Oiling and checking loose parts

If you use your bike regularly you should oil it about every two weeks. Use a good cycle oil, or dry lubricator which comes in an aerosol can. For the chain, a light grease such as petroleum jelly is best. Use oil and grease sparingly.

Put petroleum jelly on a cloth, hold it on the chain and turn the pedal to move the chain round. Check the chain is not too loose – see page 48.

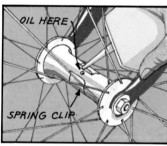

On the wheel hubs, slide round the spring clip and put a few drops of oil in the hole . Cover again with the spring clip.

The oiling point for the bottom bracket is protected by a ball-bearing. Push the bearing down and put oil in the hole.

These are the points to oil on the handlebars. Use very little oil and be careful not to get it on the handlebar grips.

Oil the central nut on the brakes, but be careful not to get any oil on the brake blocks. On rod brakes oil all the pivot points.

18

Maintenance checklist

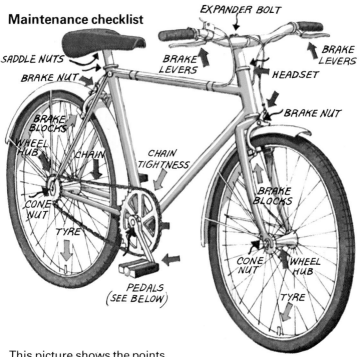

EXPANDER BOLT

SADDLE NUTS

BRAKE NUT

BRAKE LEVERS

BRAKE LEVERS

HEADSET

BRAKE NUT

BRAKE BLOCKS

WHEEL HUB

CHAIN

CHAIN TIGHTNESS

CONE NUT

TYRE

BRAKE BLOCKS

CONE NUT

WHEEL HUB

TYRE

PEDALS (SEE BELOW)

This picture shows the points you should oil regularly, the nuts you should check for looseness, and parts that should be adjusted from time-to-time.

 Oil fortnightly

Check and adjust if necessary.

Tighten nuts

Pedals

To check the pedals, hold one in each hand. If they wobble up and down, they need tightening.

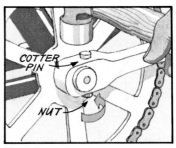

COTTER PIN

NUT

To tighten, hammer down the cotter pins, as shown here, and tighten the nuts underneath. For more information see page 41.

Mending a puncture

If you are out on the road and get a flat tyre, it may be only a slow puncture. By pumping up the tyre from time-to-time you will probably be able to get home to mend it. Never ride on a flat tyre though, or you will ruin the inner tube inside the tyre, and the tyre as well.

If it is a bad puncture you will have to try and fix it by the roadside, so always carry your puncture repair kit.

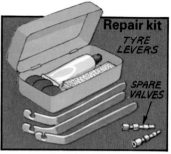

For mending punctures you need three tyre levers, glasspaper, glue and patches. You can buy all these in a kit.

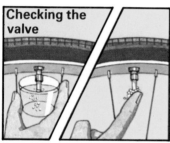

A leaking valve can cause a flat tyre. Check by holding in water or putting spit on it. If it bubbles, put in a new valve.

If the valve is alright, turn the bike upside-down and undo the wheel nuts to remove the wheel*.

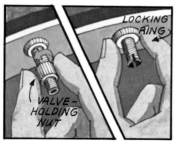

Remove the valve dustcap, the valve-holding nut and the valve. Then undo the valve-locking ring. Put them somewhere safe.

Put a tyre lever under the edge of the tyre and lift it out of the rim. Hook lever round a spoke and repeat with other levers.

*See page 49 for how to take off the back wheel.

Work round a third of the tyre with the levers, then roll it off with your hands so one edge of tyre is outside the wheel rim.

VALVE STEM

Push the valve stem out of the wheel and pull the inner tube out of the tyre. Put valve back on inner-tube and pump up.

Finding the puncture

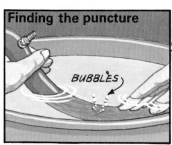

BUBBLES

To find out where the hole is, pass the tube bit-by-bit through a bowl of water. Bubbles of air escaping show where hole is.

AIR ESCAPING

If you have no water, hold the tube near your face to feel for air. To find the exact place, spit on it and look for bubbles.

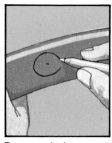

Draw a circle round the hole with a ball-point pen, then let the tube down.

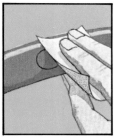

Rub the area with glasspaper, and apply glue as instructed on tube.

Press a patch firmly on the tube. Leave to dry. Then check in water again for leaks.

21

Putting the tyre back on

Before replacing the tube, look inside the tyre to make sure there is nothing which could have caused the puncture.

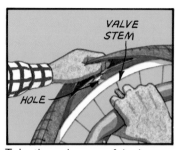

Take the valve out of the inner tube again. Then put the tube back on the wheel rim with the valve stem through the hole.

Put most of the tyre back on the wheel with your hands. Push the valve stem in to make sure the inner tube is not trapped.

Fit the last bit of tyre back with tyre levers. Refit the valve-locking ring, valve and valve-holding nut.

Pump the tyre up a little, then work round it with your hands, like this, to make sure tube is not caught under edge of tyre.

Put the wheel back on the bike and pump the tyre up as hard as you can.

22

Customizing your bike

At bicycle shops and motor accessory shops you can buy all kinds of horns, bells, mirrors, tassels, handlebar grips and many other things to fix on your bike.

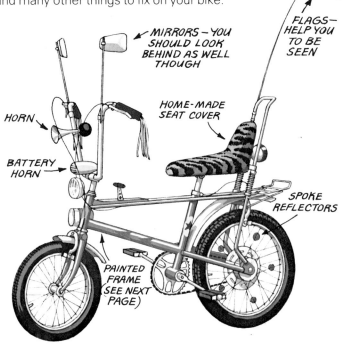

FLAGS—HELP YOU TO BE SEEN

MIRRORS — YOU SHOULD LOOK BEHIND AS WELL THOUGH

HOME-MADE SEAT COVER

HORN

BATTERY HORN

SPOKE REFLECTORS

PAINTED FRAME (SEE NEXT PAGE)

Making a seat cover

FAKE FUR FABRIC

Cut a piece of fabric large enough to fit over the seat and tuck underneath.

Turn the edge of the fabric over twice and stitch. Leave 3cm open at the end.

Thread tape or elastic through hem, pull tight round saddle and knot.

Decorating the frame

For painting, aerosol cans of metallic or metal-flake paint are best. You can also use chrome tapes and transfers. You can buy all these at motor accessory shops. You also need thick paper for making stencils for patterns, and masking tape.

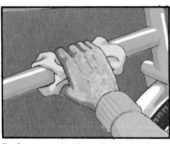

Before you paint, clean the bike frame and make sure it is free of grease and rust (see pages 16–17 and 57).

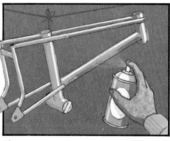

If you want to spray the frame one colour before decorating it, you should dismantle it first — see the second part of this book.

Then plan the patterns and cut the shapes out of paper to make stencils.

STENCIL MASKING TAPE

Stick the stencils on and cover all parts not to be sprayed. Spray evenly.

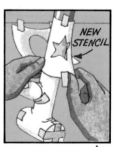

NEW STENCIL

When dry, remove the stencil and put another shape on to complete pattern.

Burglar alarm

This is an alarm to scare off bike borrowers and thieves. When they touch the seat, the horn goes off.
To make it you need a battery horn, a small on/off switch, two pieces of card covered with tin foil, a small piece of sponge, some electric flex, and a seat cover.

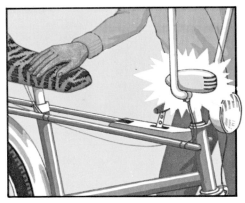

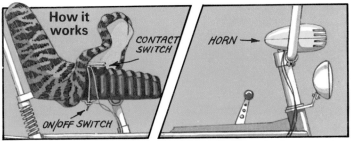

How it works

CONTACT SWITCH

ON/OFF SWITCH

HORN →

Under the seat cover there is a contact switch made of the two pieces of card with sponge between them. This is wired up to the horn.

When the burglar leans on the seat he squashes the sponge so the two bits of card touch and complete the electric circuit.

TIN FOIL OVER CARD

SPONGE

Make the contact switch like this, with a piece of flex joined to each card.

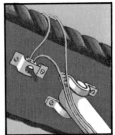

Cut one of the flexes and wire the on/off switch like this. Fix under the saddle.

Attach the wires to the horn and bolt to the handlebars.

25

Going on a cycle tour

Cycling is a good way of exploring the countryside. You can choose small back roads and get away from the traffic and even cycle along tracks and paths.

Before you go on a really long trip, it is a good idea to do some short day trips, to get used to cycling long distances. A successful trip needs to be carefully planned. Here are some ideas to help you.

For carrying your things on a day trip you need a saddle bag. Never wear a back pack as it throws you off balance.

PANNIER

For longer trips you needs bags called panniers. These hang over the wheels and do not affect your balance.

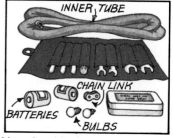

INNER TUBE

CHAIN LINK

BATTERIES BULBS

You should take some tools with you, and a puncture repair kit, spare inner tube, chain link and lamp batteries and bulbs.

Test trip

It is a good idea to make a test trip with your bike loaded up, so you can find out how far you can travel in a day.

When your bike is loaded it will be much heavier. It will take longer to stop when you brake and be harder to pedal uphill.

Planning your route

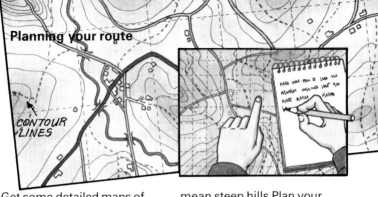

CONTOUR LINES

Get some detailed maps of where you are going and study the area. Watch out for contour lines close together which mean steep hills. Plan your route carefully and work out how far you can travel in a day, and where to stop for the night.

On long trips it is best to go with some friends, rather than by yourself. Ride single file, though, even on empty roads.

Be careful not to use up all your energy in the first few hours. You can always walk up really steep hills.

WATER BOTTLE

Take some refreshments with you. You can strap a plastic water bottle to the bike frame.

Wear loose, comfortable clothes and flat, thick-soled shoes. Take a jacket, so you are ready for any weather.

27

Racing

Racing is a popular sport for professional and amateur cyclists, and attracts huge crowds of spectators. There are many different kinds of races. Some take place on the roads, and others on specially built cycle tracks.

Racing cycles are very light with many special features to help the cyclist go faster. On pages 30–31 you can find out how to adapt your bike for racing.

Road races

The most famous road race is the *Tour de France,* across France. It covers over 2,000km and lasts three weeks.

In long races, team organizers travel behind the cyclists with food and spare wheels and bicycles for the cyclists.

Sometimes the race is divided into stages, with competitors gaining points for the fastest hill climb, or the fastest short sprint.

Time trials

In these, the cyclists start one after the other. The winner is the one who completes the route in the shortest time.

Cyclo-cross

These are races along the roads and across country. Sometimes the ground is so rough, the racers have to carry their bikes.

Track racing

Cycle tracks are short circuits with steep, banked corners. The cyclists can ride up the banks, then go down the steep part to gain speed. In long races they try not to be at the front till the end of the race, so they are sheltered by the other cyclists.

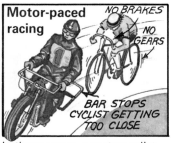

Motor-paced racing

NO BRAKES

NO GEARS

BAR STOPS CYCLIST GETTING TOO CLOSE

In these races, a motorcyclist rides in front of each cyclist. He sets the speed for the cyclist and shelters him.

Pursuit races

Two teams start at opposite ends of the track and the team which catches up with the other, or which is the fastest, wins.

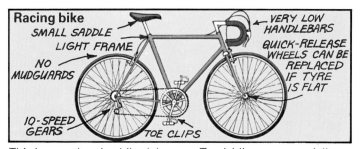

Racing bike

SMALL SADDLE

LIGHT FRAME

NO MUDGUARDS

10-SPEED GEARS

TOE CLIPS

VERY LOW HANDLEBARS

QUICK-RELEASE WHEELS CAN BE REPLACED IF TYRE IS FLAT

This is a road-racing bike. It is very light, but strong as the racer puts a lot of weight on the pedals.

Track bikes are especially strongly built. Usually they have no brakes or gears, as they are not necessary on the track.

Converting a bike for racing

These two pages show some of the adjustments you can make to an ordinary sports or touring bike to help you go faster. If you are really keen on racing though, it may be worth your while saving up to buy a proper racing bike.

When you buy spare parts for your bike, take the old part along to the bike shop to make sure you get the right type and size.

Racing position

For racing you need dropped handlebars. The low position makes you more streamlined and gives you more push on the pedals.

Converted sports bike

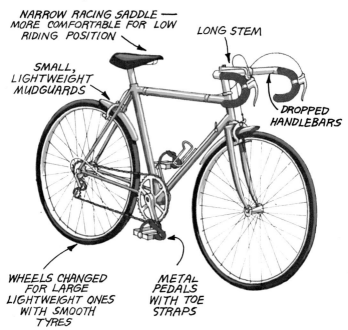

NARROW RACING SADDLE — MORE COMFORTABLE FOR LOW RIDING POSITION

LONG STEM

SMALL, LIGHTWEIGHT MUDGUARDS

DROPPED HANDLEBARS

WHEELS CHANGED FOR LARGE LIGHTWEIGHT ONES WITH SMOOTH TYRES

METAL PEDALS WITH TOE STRAPS

Changing the handlebars and stem

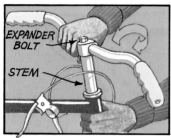

Unbolt the brake levers, then unscrew the expander bolt and tap it down as described on page 5. Pull stem out of frame.

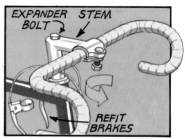

Fit the dropped handlebars into the new stem. Put the stem in the frame at the right height for you and tighten expander bolt.

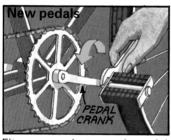

Fit a spanner between the pedal and pedal crank and unscrew the pedal. Both pedals unscrew towards the back of the bike.

Screw the lightweight metal pedals on to the pedal cranks. Fit toe straps on the pedals to give you a better grip.

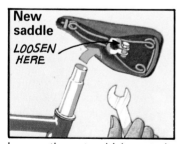

Loosen the nuts which control the angle of the seat. Remove the saddle and fit the new one. Tighten the nuts.

A flint guard stops stones damaging smooth tyres. Bolt it under the brake nuts on the front and back wheels.

31

How to race

The best way to practise racing is to join a club. The club will probably have a trainer who can help you improve your riding technique and you can race against the other members of the club to improve your speed.

If you do not join a club you could organize some races with friends. For your training, ride as often as you can, keeping in low gear so you learn how to pedal very fast.

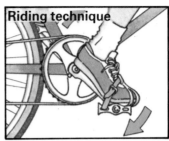

Riding technique

With toe straps on your pedals you can pull the pedals up as well as pushing them down and get more power in your pedalling.

Push and pull on the handlebars, throwing the bike from side-to-side in rhythm with your pedalling.

Learn to take corners very fast and tightly so you do not lose any speed. Lean right into the corner to keep your balance.

When cycling in a group, try not to be leader until the end of the race. This way you save energy as you are protected from wind.

Practise cycling at a good, steady pace, and going uphill without losing speed. Practise going fast on the flat too.

Some races to do

If you organize your own races, you need somewhere for the racing course where there is very little traffic. Be careful of pedestrians too.

Remember the road rules, and never break the highway code for the sake of gaining a little extra speed.

Long distance race

Choose a course about 15km long. Set off at 5 minute intervals and have someone at the finishing line to time when each of you arrives.

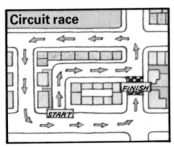

Circuit race

Plan a short circuit and set off at one minute intervals. Time when each person finishes. The one with the shortest time wins.

Elimination race

Race round a short course. At the end of each lap the last to arrive drops out. The winner is the last person left in the race.

Relay race

This is like an ordinary relay race, but on bicycles. The two teams race round the course, and the first to finish wins.

Slalom

Mark out a wiggly track for the competitors to race round. They must not touch the ground with their feet and the fastest wins.

33

Bike scrambling and trials

These are races over rough ground. You can work out a course on a rough track, or build your own obstacles to make the course more difficult.

For this kind of racing, lower the saddle on your bike so your weight is low and it is easier to balance.

Scrambling

The riders all start at the same time, and the first to finish is the winner.

Trials

Riders go one at a time and must not put their feet down. Fewest faults wins.

Riding techniques

Keep to a low gear as this gives you more control and power.

To swerve keep your body upright and push the bike to one side.

Avoid dangerous short cuts. The longer route may be shorter in the end.

Control skids by turning front wheel the same way as back wheel is skidding.

To get over a steep ridge, try to lift the front wheel on to the ridge.

When landing, pull the front wheel up, so the back wheel lands first.

34

Scrambling bike

EXTRA-WIDE HANDLEBARS FOR BETTER CONTROL

WIDE, COMFORTABLE SEAT

RACE NUMBER

6

RUBBER PEDALS— SAFER IF YOU FALL OFF

BIG MUDGUARDS AND FLAPS

6

THICK STUDDED TYRES

Here are some things you can do to a bike to make it more stable for scrambling.

MUDDY PUDDLE

ROCKS

LOGS

RIDGE

On a scrambling track, have lots of different kinds of obstacles, but not too close to each other, or you will never pick up speed.

For a trials track, the obstacles can be as complicated and as close together as you like.

Basic guidelines

This part of the book shows you how to take a bike apart so you can grease the bearings, or fit new parts. To keep a bike in good working order the parts should be greased about twice a year. If your bike is not running well, though, turn to the fault-finding guide on pages 60–62 to find out what may be wrong.

If you decide to do your own bike maintenance, you will need most of the tools shown on the opposite page.

Some of the parts on your bike may be a bit different from those in the pictures and instructions on the following pages, but they still work in the same way. Before you take the bike apart, always look at how the pieces fit together so you know exactly how to put them back again.

Make lists of parts as you undo them, so you know the order to put them back. Keep them safe in labelled jars and egg-boxes.

If you have to replace a part, look for a name and size on it, or take it along to the cycle shop so you can match it.

Tool kit

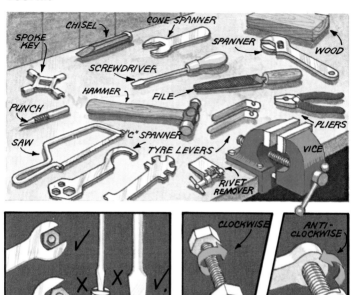

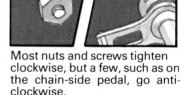

Use the right sized tools on nuts or screws, or the heads will break. A spanner should fit the sides of the nut.

Most nuts and screws tighten clockwise, but a few, such as on the chain-side pedal, go anti-clockwise.

For lubricating parts use cycle oil, and for bearings general purpose grease. Penetrating oil helps loosen nuts.

To clean greasy parts put paraffin in an old can and hold parts in a seive or a yogurt pot with holes in.

37

Fixing cable brakes

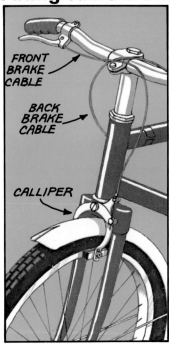

FRONT BRAKE CABLE

BACK BRAKE CABLE

CALLIPER

These two pages show how to replace the brake blocks when they are worn down, and how to fit a new cable.

Fitting brake blocks

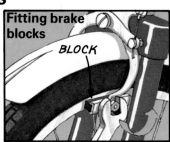

BLOCK

Remove the old blocks and shoes by undoing the nut as shown. You can buy new blocks with or without the metal shoes.

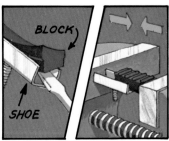

BLOCK

SHOE

If you buy only the blocks, lever the old ones out of the shoes and tap the new ones in with a hammer, or slide in with a vice.

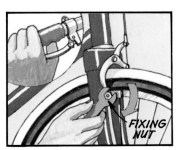

FIXING NUT

Fit the shoe back on the calliper and line the block up with the wheel rim. Hold the brake lever on while you tighten the nut.

Cable replacement

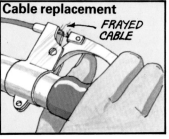

FRAYED CABLE

If the cable is frayed you need to fit a new one. You can buy cable in plastic casing, or slide new cable into old casing.

Removing old cable

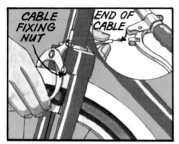

Hold brake lever on and brake block against wheel rim. Let go of brake lever and slide out the cable. Undo cable fixing nut on calliper to free other end.

Fit new cable to the brake lever first, then to the calliper. Hold block against wheel rim while tightening cable fixing nut. Adjust brakes as on page 17.

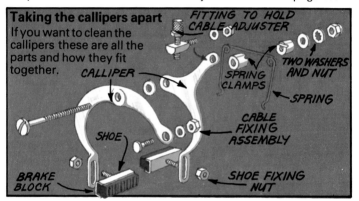

Taking the callipers apart

If you want to clean the callipers these are all the parts and how they fit together.

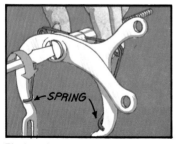

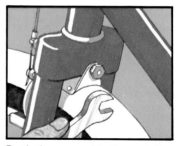

Fit the pieces together as above, with the spring round the callipers. Tighten the screw gently.

Push the assembly through the bike frame. Put the mudguard fitting on the screw, then fit the washer and nut.

Rod brakes

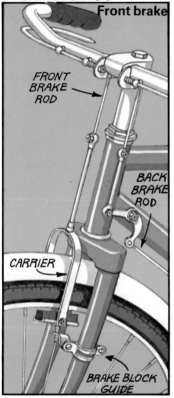

Front brake

FRONT BRAKE ROD

BACK BRAKE ROD

CARRIER

BRAKE BLOCK GUIDE

On this type of brakes, the brake blocks are connected to the brake levers by a system of rods, and the blocks press on the underside of the wheel rim. They are more tricky to adjust than cable brakes.

The brake blocks should be 3mm below the wheel rim. If you have to adjust them, start at the wheel end. Loosen each nut and adjust the length of the rods, working your way up to the brake levers.

Back brake

REAR BRAKE BLOCK ADJUSTER

BRAKE BLOCK GUIDE

Replacing brake blocks

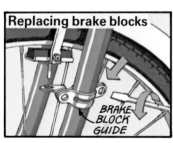

BRAKE BLOCK GUIDE

Loosen the screws on the brake block guide and slide it down the frame to free the brake block shoe.

FIXING NUT REMOVED

Undo fixing nut holding shoe to carrier. Pull shoe out of carrier and fit new blocks as for cable brakes, page 38.

Fixing wobbly pedals

Wobbly pedals are caused by worn and loose cotter pins holding the pedal cranks to the bottom bracket. You can fix them by knocking the pins down and doing up the nuts, as shown on page 19. If there is no pin left to knock down, you have to fit new ones.

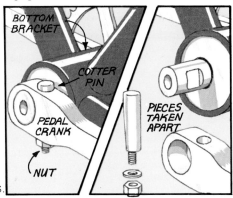

Remove the nut on the end of the cotter pin and tap the pin down flush with the pedal. Then tap it out with a punch.

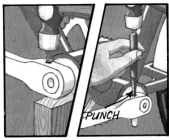

Press the new pin in. If too little of the pin sticks out to fit the nut, file a little off the flat side of the cotter pin.

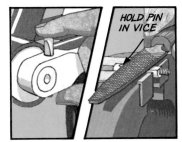

Check the pins are the right way up, as shown here, before fitting the nuts.

Then hammer them down far enough to fit the nuts on the ends.

Screw the nuts on gently. Do not overtighten or you will strip the threads.

Greasing pedals

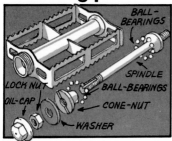

These are all the pieces inside the pedals. About twice a year you should clean and grease the ball bearings.

Unscrew each pedal with a spanner between the pedal and the crank. Both pedals unscrew towards the back of the bike.

Unscrew the oil-cap, being careful not to squash it.

Then remove the lock nut. You may need a very narrow spanner to reach it.

Lift the washer out. It has a ridge which fits in a groove in the spindle.

Unscrew the cone nut by pushing with a screwdriver in the slots.

Then tip the ball-bearings into paraffin to clean them.

Pull the spindle out and clean the other bearings and all the parts in paraffin.

Putting them back together

Put a little grease in the space for the bearings. Press them into the grease.

Put spindle in and put grease and the other ball-bearings in other end of pedal.

Screw on the cone nut and tighten. Make sure pedal turns freely on spindle.

Drop the washer into place and refit the lock nut. Check pedal still turns freely.

Put a little grease in the oil-cap and screw on. Careful not to get the thread crossed.

Fit the pedal back on the crank. Both pedals screw on towards the front of the bike.

Unscrew oil-cap and two nuts holding end-plate. Remove end-plate.

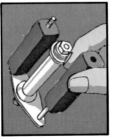

Pull the old, worn rubbers off the pedals.

Slip the new rubbers on, then replace end-plate, nuts and oil-cap.

43

Cleaning the bottom bracket

The bottom bracket contains the spindle which turns with the pedals. If the spindle and the ball-bearings around it get dirty or dry, the pedals make a grating noise as you cycle.

The pictures on these pages show how to take apart the bottom bracket so you can clean and grease the parts. If the bearings are worn, take them to a bicycle shop to match them when you replace them.

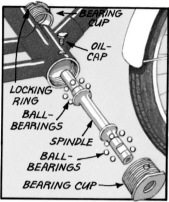

Take the pedals and cranks off by removing the nuts from the cotter pins and knocking the pins out.

Undo the locking ring with a "C" spanner, or tap it carefully with a chisel or screwdriver to loosen it.

If there is an oil-cap undo it with a small spanner.

Then undo the bearing cup with a special spanner, or a punch and hammer.

Tip bearings and spindle out and put them in paraffin to clean them.

Unscrew the other bearing cup with a big spanner and clean in paraffin.

Replace the first bearing cup and screw it in as far as it will go.

Put some grease inside the cup and push the ball-bearings into it.

Put the spindle in from the other side. Careful not to knock ball-bearings out.

Put grease in the other bearing cup and press bearings into the grease.

Hold the spindle in the right position and put the bearing cup back on.

Tighten the bearing cup and check the spindle turns freely.

Refit the oil-cap and put the locking ring back on and tighten it.

Put the pedal cranks back on and refit the cotter pins.

Cleaning the headset

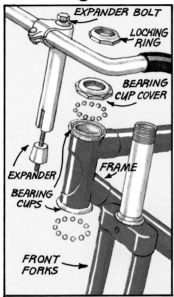

EXPANDER BOLT
LOCKING RING
BEARING CUP COVER
EXPANDER
FRAME
BEARING CUPS
FRONT FORKS

These are the parts inside the headset. The ball-bearings allow the handlebars and front forks to turn freely inside the frame. If you hear a grating noise when you turn the handlebars, the bearings need cleaning and greasing.

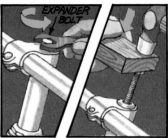

EXPANDER BOLT

Take the handlebars off by undoing the expander bolt 25mm, then tapping it down. The handlebars will then lift out.

LOCKING RING

Undo the locking ring on top of the frame with a spanner or a "C" spanner, or tap it with a hammer and punch.

BEARING CUP COVER

Loosen bearing cup cover. Turn bike over, unscrew cup and tip bearings out.

FRAME

Pull the front forks out of the frame, being careful not to lose any bearings.

BEARING CUP

Then pick the ball-bearings out of the bearing cup and clean all parts.

46

Putting the headset back together

Grease the bearing cup at bottom end of frame and put ball-bearings in.

Slide the front forks into the frame and fit the locking ring to hold them in place.

Turn bike over. Take locking ring off again. Grease bearing cup and put bearings in.

Screw on bearing cup cover. Tighten by hand. Make sure front forks turn.

Put the locking ring on and tighten with a spanner, or tap with a punch as before.

Make sure the front forks still turn freely and loosen the locking ring if not.

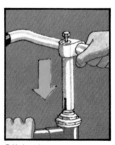

Slide the handlebars back into the frame.

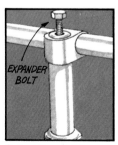

Set at the right height for you and pull up the expander bolt.

Tighten the expander bolt.

47

Fitting a new chain

A chain gradually stretches and wears down. If it becomes too big it may come off while you are cycling*. If your chain is too long you can adjust it or fit a new one, as shown here. A dry, dirty chain wears down more quickly, so keep it lightly greased.

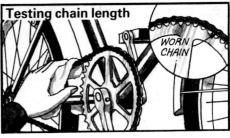
Testing chain length

WORN CHAIN

When you press on the chain, like this, it should go down only about 12mm. The chain should also fit right into the teeth of the chain wheel.

Adjusting the chain

Loosen the back wheel nuts. Slide wheel back a little. Tighten wheel nuts.

Fitting a new chain

CONNECTING LINK

Find the connecting link and lever it off to remove the chain.

RIVETING TOOL

With derailleur gears you have to remove a rivet with a riveting tool to get chain off.

Test the length of the new chain. If too long, remove rivets to take off links.

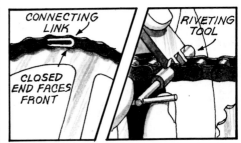
CONNECTING LINK

CLOSED END FACES FRONT

RIVETING TOOL

Put the chain round the chain wheel and sprocket and join it with the connecting link or if it is a derailleur chain, use the riveting tool to replace the rivet.

For putting it back on, see page 61.

How to take off the back wheel

With hub gears

Unscrew the gear change cable from the back wheel.

Adjust the brake blocks so the wheel can pass betwen them.

Loosen the wheel nuts on both sides of the wheel.

Slide the wheel forwards, lift the chain off and pull wheel up and out.

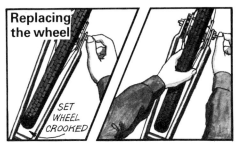

Replacing the wheel

SET WHEEL CROOKED

Put the chain on and fit the wheel in the forks. Set the wheel crooked and tighten the wheel nuts. Then push the wheel to straighten it and tension the chain. Tighten nuts.

Derailleur

Set gears so chain is on the smallest sprocket and undo the wheel nuts.

Push the chain guide forward to free the chain.

Hold the chain like this and slide the wheel up and out. Refit as for hub gears.

49

Cleaning the wheel bearings

Inside the hubs of the wheels there is a spindle and ball-bearings which need to be kept clean and greased, as shown on these two pages. If they are dirty and dry, the wheels make a crunching noise as they turn.

If the wheels get bent, or you break a spoke, it is best to take them to a cycle shop for repair. For tightening the spokes, or fitting a new rim tape inside the wheel rim, see page 55.

Turn the bike upside-down and loosen the wheel nuts to take off the wheels. For removing back wheel, see previous page.

Take the wheel nuts right off. Beneath them are the lock nuts.

Unscrew both the lock nuts at the same time, with two spanners in opposite directions, or wrap other end of spindle in a cloth and clamp in a vice while you undo it.

The cone nut at one end of the spindle has flat sides. Unscrew this one.

Turn the wheel over and with your hand under the hub, pull out the spindle. Put the ball-bearings in paraffin to clean, and poke out any which are stuck inside the hub.

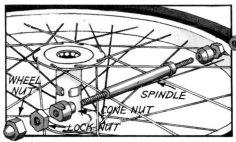

If it comes off, take the cone nut off the other end of the spindle. Clean all the nuts and bearings in paraffin. If any are worn or pitted, replace them.

Next, put grease in one side of the wheel and press the ball-bearings in.

Put flat-sided cone nut, and lock nut, on spindle and put in wheel.

Hold the spindle and turn the wheel over at a slant, like this.

Put grease and bearings in other side of hub. Screw on the cone and lock nut.

Hold spindle and tighten flat-sided cone so wheel turns smoothly.

Tighten both the lock nuts together and check wheel still turns smoothly.

Put the wheel back on the bike, centring it between the forks. Replace wheel nuts.

Adjusting hub gears and . . .

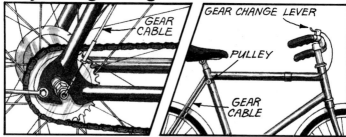

These are hidden inside the hub of the back wheel. You should oil the wheel hub about once a month, and also the pulley which carries the gear cable to the gear-change lever. If the gears are not working properly, adjust the length of the cable.

Adjusting faulty gears

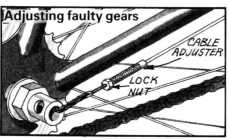

To lengthen the cable, unscrew the lock nut then unscrew the cable adjuster. To tighten the cable, move the cable adjuster up, then tighten the lock nut.

Set the gear lever to the middle speed (usually 2 or N).

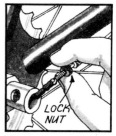

You should see the last link of the gear chain in hole where it joins the hub.

Turn the cable adjuster until the link is in the correct position.

Then set gear lever to high (3 or H) and screw lock nut up to cable adjuster.

derailleur gears

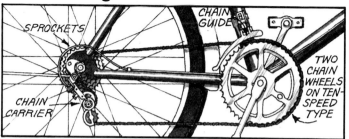

These have five different sized sprockets at the back and a chain carrier to guide the chain on to the different sprockets. The ten-speed type has two chain wheels at the front and a chain guide to carry the chain. If the chain does not sit properly on the sprockets or wheels, it needs adjusting.

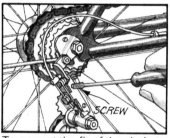

To correct the fit of the chain to the sprockets, set the gears so the chain is on the largest sprocket. Then adjust the top screw in the chain guide*.

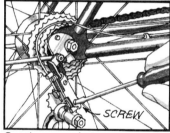

Set the gears in top gear so the chain is on the smallest sprocket and adjust the lower screw until the chain fits properly on the sprocket.

With ten-speed gears, check that the chain carrier is not rubbing against the chain and that chain sits properly on both chain wheels. Adjust by means of screws on top.

Check, too, that screws holding gear levers are tight so gears do not slip.

*Check the instructions for your gears if they are different from these.

Checking dynamo lamps

The power for these lamps is made as you pedal along. There are two types: hub units and tyre-driven units. Hub units should be taken to a dealer for repair. Tyre-driven units should be correctly positioned, as shown below.

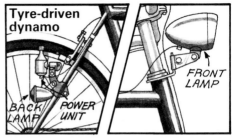

Tyre-driven dynamo

BACK LAMP
POWER UNIT
FRONT LAMP

The power unit can be on the front or back tyre. If it is not correctly positioned, you will not get a good, even light, and it may also wear away the tyre.

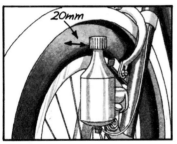

20mm

When it is off, the top of the dynamo should be 20mm from the tyre. To adjust, loosen screw holding unit to the frame.

BOLT

The centre of the dynamo unit should be directly above the centre of the wheel. To adjust, loosen angle-adjusting bolt.

Hub unit

If it is not working, test the dynamo by fixing two wires and a bulb to the hub. If the bulb lights when you turn the wheel, the dynamo is alright and lamp bulbs need replacing.

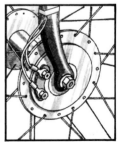

Check wires are connected to hub. If it still does not work, take to a dealer.

54

Fixing spokes and rim tapes

Loose or broken spokes may cause the wheel to lose its shape. You can fit new ones on the front wheel, but those on the back are best done at a cycle shop.

The rim tape inside the wheel rim protects the inner tube from the ends of the spokes.

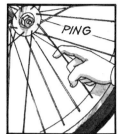
Pluck the spokes to see if they are loose. They should make a clear pinging noise.

You can gently tighten loose spokes with a spoke key, like this.

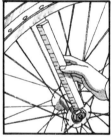
To replace a spoke, measure the length you need and buy one the right length.

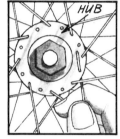
Thread through hub, lace through other spokes, out through rim.

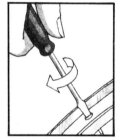
Tighten the screw in the top of the spoke and tension with a spoke key.

Fitting a new rim tape

If the tape is rotten and worn, or very creased, you should fit a new one.

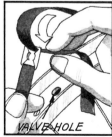
Put the new tape round the wheel, threading the buckle like this.

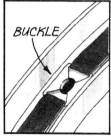
Pull the tape tight and make sure the buckle sits flat over the valve hole.

Renovating an old bike

One of the cheapest ways to get yourself a bike is to ask around and see if anyone has an old one in their garage or shed. Even if a bike looks in a very bad condition, you can probably put it right with some work. As well as checking the points mentioned on the next four pages you should grease all the bearings, as described in the maintenance section of this book.

First clean the bike with paraffin to get rid of grease and see what state it is in.

Then dismantle the bike. On wheels, use a spanner on both sides at the same time.

To loosen very rusty screws, put penetrating oil on them and leave it to sink in.

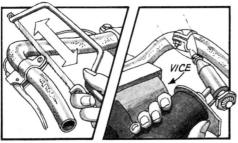

If you still cannot undo the screws you can saw through them with a hack-saw, or heat with a blow-lamp, then oil and leave to cool. A garage would probably do this for you.

After dismantling, clean all the parts and store in labelled containers.

Repainting the frame

The frame will probably be very rusty and may even need repainting. To remove rust you need a wire brush or steel wool, and rust preventer which you can buy at motor shops. If the frame has any cracks or holes, these should be welded. A garage would do this for you.

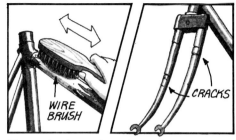

Clamp the frame in a vice, or hang it up and cover any parts you did not manage to remove, with plastic bags. Brush off the rust and loose paint and examine for cracks.

Treat the rusty parts with rust preventer following the instructions.

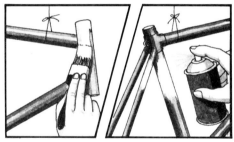

Brush-on paint is best for very uneven surfaces, but spray gives a better finish on smooth surfaces. Test the spray on a small area to check it does not cause bubbling.

If you want to decorate the frame, see page 24 for how to do it.

After painting, put a few drops of oil inside the frame to stop it rusting.

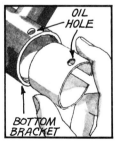

Cut up a plastic bottle and put it in the bottom bracket so rust cannot get in.

RENOVATING AN OLD BIKE
Chrome

Chrome is a hard covering on the steel frame. If the chrome is rusty it means it is scratched and the steel underneath has rusted. To remove the rust you need steel wool or you can treat it with rust preventer from a motor shop.

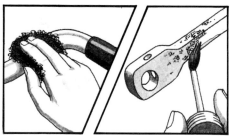

Rub the rusty parts of the chrome very hard with steel wool. If the rust is very bad and the chrome has flaked off, you will need to paint it with rust preventer.

If you rub off most of the chrome, paint the part to stop more rust.

You can put sticky handlebar tape on handlebars instead of painting them.

To protect clean chrome, polish it with household polish or car wax.

Brake fittings

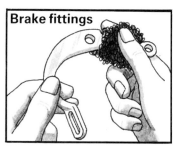

These are made of alloy and do not go rusty. White spots can be rubbed off with steel wool. Clean with metal polish.

Saddle

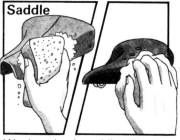

Wash a plastic saddle with soapy water and polish leather with saddle soap or neutral polish. Rub the polish off well.

Wheels

If the wheels are very rusty or buckled it is best to replace them. Wheels are made in different sizes and rim types, so take the old ones to the shop to match them.

You can tighten and replace spokes as described on page 55, but spokes on the back wheel are best left to a dealer.

On a very old bike the tyres and inner tubes will have rotted and need replacing.

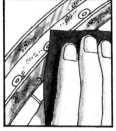

Clean rust off wheel rims with emery paper. They must be smooth for braking.

Fitting new mudguards

Put the mudguards through the forks and do all the nuts up loosely.

Then fit the wheel and adjust the mudguard so it does not rub on the wheel.

MUDGUARD STAY

Tighten the nuts and saw off the ends of the mudguard stays. File ends smooth.

Putting the bike together

After cleaning all the parts and replacing any broken ones you can put the bike back together again. Follow the instructions in the maintenance part of this book, keeping all the parts clean and greasing the bearings with general purpose grease.

Fault-finding guide

If you are not sure what is wrong with your bike, see if the problem is mentioned on the next three pages. These pages show you what may be wrong and give ideas for putting it right.

Check the brake nut in case it is loose. Use a screwdriver on the front and a spanner on the back at the same time.

Bike judders when you brake

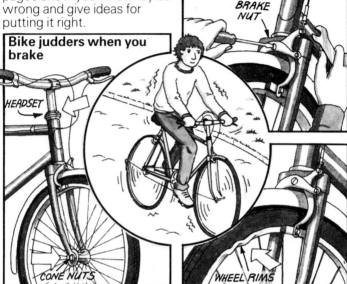

Make sure the cone nuts (see page 50) and the headset (see page 46) have not come loose. Do not tighten them too much.

Look at your wheel rims. If they are badly buckled, or very rough and rusty, take them to a dealer for advice.

Check the brake blocks. They may have worn away and need replacing.

Make sure the brake cables or rods are not too loose.

Seat tilts and swivels

Tighten nuts under saddle to stop it swivelling, and on stem to stop tilting.

Brake levers slip

HANDLEBAR TAPE

Put handlebar tape under brake lever fixtures to give them something to grip on.

Handlebars slip

EXPANDER BOLT

Make sure the expander bolt is working and tighten it up.

Crunching noises from wheels, bottom bracket, steering or pedals

This usually means the bearings inside are dirty and dry. If you oil them in the normal way, the noise will probably stop, but it is best to dismantle the part and clean and grease the bearings, as described in the maintenance part of this book.

CYCLE OIL

GREASE

Chain comes off

The chain may be too loose. See page 48 for adjusting and fitting a new chain.

To replace, put it over the back sprocket and turn wheel backwards.

Then hook over chain wheel. Lift back wheel and turn pedal forwards.

Loose chain wheel

Usually caused by loose bearing cups in bottom bracket. See page 44 and tighten.

Bent pedals

If the pedals are bent it is best to fit new ones.

Loose pedals

Knock down the cotter pins and tighten the nuts, see page 41.

Rubbing noises

Wheel is off-centre and rubbing on mudguard. See page 49 for centring.

Brake blocks rubbing on tyres. See page 17 for how to adjust blocks.

Mudguard is rubbing on wheel. See page 5 for adjusting mudguard.

Bumpy tyres

The inner tube is not properly positioned round valve or may be about to burst.

Rattles

Some nuts and bolts, such as those on the mudguards, continually work loose. To stop this you can put locking fluid, from a hardware store, on them to hold them tight.

First aid

Just in case you do fall off your bike, or are with someone who does, it is a good idea to know what to do.

If you are a bit shocked after a fall, sit down for a few minutes to relax. Then check your bike to make sure nothing is damaged before you ride on.

If you go on a cycle tour it is best to go in a group of three and to tell someone where you are going.

After a fall, get yourself and your bike out of the road as quickly as possible in case a car comes along.

When you get home bathe cuts and grazes, put antiseptic on them and cover cuts with sticky plaster.

If you are with someone who is badly hurt, do not move them unless it is really necessary as this can make their injuries worse.

Cover them with clothes to keep them warm. Direct traffic round them.

If there is a bad wound, press it with a cloth or your hands to stop bleeding.

Call an ambulance as soon as possible. Then stay with the injured person.

63

Index